D1158421

Edgar Allan's MURDER

Insights into a Crow's World
by

ALICE WHEATLAND INGRAHAM

Edgar Allan's Murder, Insights into a Crow's World

Copyright © 2012 by Alice Wheatland Ingraham

ISBN: 978-1-936447-67-1

Designed by Maine Authors Publishing, Rockland, Maine

www.MaineAuthorsPublishing.com

photographs courtesty of David Elliott

Dedicated to
The Young at Heart

CONTENTS

INTRODUCTION

I don't beg for your approval. I simply wish to be recognized, as does everyone else. I have been at various times ignored, accused falsely of wrongdoing and denounced as a trespasser. However, by well-informed folk, I am held in high esteem. I ask now for judgment that is based on fact rather than unsubstantiated supposition or gossip. Respect is the due of all beings, myself included. My fascinating friend, Alice Ingraham, offered a quote from the writer, Ralph Waldo Emerson, to assuage my troubled thoughts; "To be great is to be misunderstood". Similarly, Elizabeth Barrett Browning wrote: "So huge the chasm between the false and the true". I hope that you will become enlightened and fascinated by the following erudite presentation that Alice has aided me in offering.

My name is Edgar Allan. I'm a handsome ebony male. I'm robust, dignified, courageous, agile, and utterly egotistical. I have abilities beyond most people's imaginings. My vision is extremely acute, as is my hearing. I have strong legs and a stout (but not obese) body. My stentorian voice is seldom ignored. I do have a tendency to be rather nervous and suspicious. I can be imperious and, when necessary, duplicitous. Humble, I am not. (I believe that arrogance can present itself truthfully and altruistically.) I am shrewd and experienced. I'm a seasoned veteran of conflict, an effective aviator, and a brave, aggressive strategist. I'll defend my society to the death. As a matter of fact, I'm often invited to participate in wars that otherwise wouldn't involve my own kinsmen. Because of my wisdom, mental acuity, and innate leadership capabilities, I've earned the honor of being the general and sovereign potentate of my society.

That's enough about me for the moment. I should tell you about my friend Alice, who has taken my story upon herself. She has earned my trust and tentative respect. She's comely, sensitive, and not very social. I understand; I too prefer the company of my closest group and family members. I'm glad of the latter, since I don't much like *her* friends. They're too aggressive, can't communicate with me, and interrupt me and my companions incessantly. They stare at me impolitely. Alice's own family is more tolerable. The little ones don't jabber at all. They do *remind* me, though, of my own offspring, imploring vociferously for food. Ben and Elsa, Alice's other third generation younglings, are OK, too. Alice reminds them to move slowly and speak softly when we are around. I appreciate that they like me. As Alice and I become more and more familiar with each other I think she will prove to be a valuable ally. She comes when I call (as any female friend of mine should!). She's attentive to what I say and is learning to speak my native tongue. She doesn't pester me when I'm busy-though I catch her watching me during the day and sometimes she follows me around. I don't mind, I find her attention flattering. (My only pet peeve is her camera.) We have picnic brunches together nearly every day except during blizzards, Nor'easters, Sou'westers, hurricanes, no-name storms, perfect storms, tsunamis, earthquakes, purple squalls and overhead thunderstorms, when neither one of us feels like exposing ourselves to the elements. (Alice becomes frantic when lightning is close)!

I try to wake Alice in the morning for breakfast (I'm a dawn riser) but she never responds that early, even though I make as much noise as I can! She does know that I have a ravenous appetite and remembers what my favorite food choices are, though her attendance isn't always timely. She gets distracted and misinterprets her priorities. In my opinion, females, notably the ones past their prime, are sometimes unreliable and don't multi-task well. Alice has apologized to me, saying that she has "too much on her plate." That's not true, as I've *never* seen much on her plate! I feel slighted at those times, but I forgive and forget. When Alice can't take her meal with me, my life partner keeps me company. I eat first and she eats second. The rest of my tribe dines after us. While they are preoccupied, I remain close to make sure there are no problems. My homeland is sometimes as dangerous as is yours, but *we* don't carry lethal weapons. Our disputes are settled with more clemency.

But I've digressed. My female is gentle, accepts her role, and shows me much deference. As do many of her sex, she becomes persnickety and standoffish once in a while. I do, too (don't you?) but it's with just cause. I make a magnanimous effort to oblige her whims. I seldom rebuke her. Together, we have one very important goal in life: to have many offspring. She's a superb mother. Her birth name is Theresa, but I've nicknamed her "Tatters" because on occasion she neglects her preening. Perhaps that's one reason why Alice is fond of her: Alice doesn't much care about looking "la-di-da" either.

At the moment, I'm pleased with myself and my minions. I take my noble responsibilities seriously. It's a demanding, often rewarding and sometimes frightening role. Being vigilantly attentive can be wearing. Your president's hair turns gray or white after only a year in office! Luckily, mine doesn't, but after about five years, I'll turn my position over to another patriarch. Alice found a line by William Shakespeare that we both feel is appropriate: "Uneasy is the head that wears a crown."

Oh, I forgot to tell you: my full name is Edgar Allan Crow, crow being the operative word. I am, specifically, an American crow, the type you most often see in New England. (My territory is on Cousins Island in Yarmouth, Maine.) We are of the genus Corvus *brachyrhynchos.* Alice thinks that sounds a bit *Mafioso,* but I'm not the one who came up with the designation. However, in keeping with that thought, all "Corvus" groups, including mine, are called "murders." Most humans refer to our gatherings as "flocks." They're in error.

Alice and I will present you with an overview of our corvid attributes, a brief genealogical evolution, and a history of our behavior, our social anomalies, procreation, and unique language. Her affirmation of my need to be understood, and her communications with me, have been truly productive. (Her accent isn't quite right, but she's making progress.) Hence, I offer here an accounting of my species with the hope that you will become enthusiastic promoters of my eminence! Please stop harassing me; What's with your scarecrows, anyway? No mentally capable crow feels intimidated by, literally, a stuffed shirt!...At least, not for long. And your fake owls...we learn swiftly that they don't react to us in any way. A *living* owl is dangerous.

EVOLUTION AND COMMUNICATION

Alice's research, gleaned from many books and her computer, and organized into appropriate form, an ability that I honor her for, (along with her dedication) has informed us that birdlike creatures existed long before her own Homosapien's ancestors! Fossils indicate that *Aves* predecessors (that includes mine) lived 70 million years ago during the upper Cretaceous period, (the last period of the Mesozoic era) originating in what is now Australia and subsequently branching throughout Asia. Some crossed the Bering Land Bridge to "our" North America during the Pleistocene Epoch, less than two million years ago. Ravens crossed before we did, as they were larger, stronger, and aggressively adept at securing food killed by wolves, saber-toothed cats, and other ancient creatures that migrated during the same period. In effect, they paved the way for us crows, and I, for one, am grateful. There is paleontological evidence that crows, notably American and Fish Crows, did indeed inhabit North America during the Pleistocene period.

Corvidae found coniferous and deciduous trees and green landscapes that provided climates, food, and shelter suitable for avian survival. Though our ancestors seldom nested in them, the bogs within their territories were also beneficial. They provided (as they still do) aquatic delicacies, insects, arthropods, amphibians, sometimes dead rodents, and safety from marauding animals. No sane wolf or wild feline would choose to muck around in a bog to catch us.

My murder and I still prefer some of the same kinds of environments and food sources, among others. We still follow wolves, foxes, coyotes, and other carnivores to eat the leftovers of their kills. (We have been nicknamed wolf birds by some northeastern rural inhabitants.)

Alice's neighborhood, roughly three quarters of a square mile of Cousins Island, is perfect for our needs. We have staked out this territory as our own. It includes the requisite salt marshes, tidal flats, ponds and springs, plenty of fodder, some very tall, old evergreen woodlands, fresh spring ponds, vernal pools, lawns harboring grubs, and only a few cats. (There was a particularly lethal one last summer but he's now eternally resting.)

As for the rest of the ancient world, birdlike creatures didn't inhabit the American mid-and northwest, covered for eons by glaciers, until much later. None settled in either of the arctic regions, as those frozen tundras weren't life-supporting (although Common Ravens do now live in those realms where temperatures can dive lower than minus 40 degrees F. Our black feathers absorb the sun's warmth even during cold months.) Corvidae historically avoided the steamy regions of the extreme tropics. As our ranges expanded, however, we evolved according to our environments. To this day, Fish Crows are indigenous to Florida, and range from there to Texas. The White Necked Crow inhabits Haiti and Puerto Rico. Jamaican Crows live, you guessed it, in Jamaica. Hooded Crows live in Europe and have expanded into Egypt. There are Little Crows and Little Ravens in Australia, the Forest Raven in Tasmania, the Pied Crow in Africa and the Jungle Crow of India and Burma, to name only a few. Corvidae have been adaptable. Fossils in Porcupine Cave, Colorado, uncovered by a paleontologist named Steve Emslie, provided evidence of crow presence there roughly 1.6 million years ago. (Marzluff & Angell: *In The Company of Crows and Ravens*).

Many people think that birds are mammals, but we're not! Alice's sagacious friend, Jim Thatcher, reminded her that mammals grow their young internally. I wouldn't want my mate to carry our young in her stomach, or breastfeed them as mammals do, because they're too demanding, quarrelsome, and fidgety. Imagine how prickly and itchy their developing feather shafts would be!

Crows (Corvus brachyrhynchos), ravens and our cousins the magpies, stellar jays, jackdaws, rooks, et al., are, in fact, classed as songbirds! Truly! Our corvid communications have been said to sound like quarks-think "QuOOOrrrk!" or like gutterings, soft throaty gargling, and raucous, ear-piercing squawks. In my opinion, these accusations are significantly disrespectful and unnecessarily disparaging! We may not be melodic, but I consider us singers. We are nearly operatic and our ability to project is magnificent! *We* admire our voices. Whether you do or not is immaterial to us. Through my direction, Alice will explain this as follows:

Crows and ravens have six pairs of muscles that our voice boxes use to make a variety of sounds. "Sweety-tweety" songbird recitatives don't conform to our specific vocal anatomy and I'm glad of that. Imagine a proud, large black bird such as I, warbling! However, we have a sophisticated language (you must stop to listen sometime) and accompanying postures and gestures. You'll see us pump up and down, raise and lower our bodies and heads, flick, extend and close our wings, clack our beaks, spread and constrict our tail feathers, etc., when we want to emphasize our communications. Alice can see by our posturing what our calls are, even when she's in her house and can't hear us.

Being birds, we can see more colors and environmental details than most other animals, including humans. Because of our facial anatomy, we focus with one eye at a time. I turn my head sideways when I want to look directly at Alice. She turns her head a bit, too, but she uses both of her eyes. It means "There you are! What are you doing?" We often use combinations of calls and/ or string syllables together. Everything we say has a purpose. There are no *ums* for us nor use of the word *like* in nearly every sentence.

Our raven cousins have demonstrated that they can imitate owls hooting, chickens clucking, human whistles, babies mewling and shrieking, and even words and short sentences. Their language is diverse and sophisticated. Though we crows are much less vocally agile, our language is complex: many of our calls, and sequences of same, have several different meanings, and we accompany these messages with specific postures. These postures also have meanings when used in silence. Each murder has its own dialect, its own unique group calls. We also share common communications with other groups. Ornithologists say that if a person spends some time listening, as Alice does, you might be able to recognize about twenty basic calls that can vary in intensity, duration, rate, sequence, and pitch...and even emotion, though those twenty are only a fraction of the extent of our vocabulary. Alice can change her volume and interject pauses, even change notes, to speak rudimentarily with us. Having perfect pitch, she has noticed that I usually use the note of G (C major scale) unless I'm excited, being tender, or need to stress a message. Tatters will often use that same note, and when we duet we rarely interrupt each other. When we are attacking an enemy, though, we intensify our anger by launching a communal clamor. Our high-pitched, long-winded, projected "Ko"s warn others of a predator and its location. That's not unusual for any social and vocal creature, is it? Actually, any truly loud call means "pay attention!" We squall or shriek to emphasize that we are extremely excited, hurt, or dying. (You do the same.) Our murder members respond by attending and comforting us with soothing sounds. One or two "Kaows" mean "be silent", fly away and hide without attracting attention. We also use sounds to warn intruders to leave our territory. We are all able to express emotions such as anger, defiance, fear, affection, etc., to define home territory and to summon murder members and other Corvid neighbors for communal defense or combat. We have vocalizations to inform others of roosting locations, (especially in winter,) to announce one's own location, and to lure mates and "whisper" affection to them. We have calls to notify our members that we've found food. We are indeed a sophisticated and loquacious species.

Quoting John M. Marzluff and Tony Angell, the authors of *In The Company of Crows and Ravens,* pg. 201.

Crows utter a variety of sounds that vary in duration, harmonic structure, intensity and vibrato. By recording vocalizing crows under a variety of situations, analyzing these calls with a computer, and playing different calls to wild and captive crows, researchers are beginning to understand these call elements. One study documented twenty-three types of calls, many of which Cynthia Sims Parr later subdivided in her splendid investigation of American Crow cawing. Taken together, these studies suggest that American Crows have upward of thirty or more distinct building blocks for their Communication system.

Alice and I often exchange our three-caw, territorial greeting as well as the assembly "I'm here" caw. She's even learning modulation, tone differences, and the gargle and chirr (like a cat's loud purr and/or a chipmunk's quiet chittering) vocals. We recognize each other's voices. The members of my murder also know my voice and, because I'm their leader, don't ignore my messages. They attend to my summonses, warnings, information, etc., with alacrity, almost always.

LEGENDS AND FOLKLORE

My kind may currently be disrespected (inherited prejudice?), but in previous eras, we were held in high esteem.

It is believed that Paleolithic people recognized, even venerated, Corvids. Our images can be seen in carvings on ancient Middle East tombs. Cave art and early legends reveal respect for our intelligence. The "ancients" were perceptive.

Alice related to me that a book called the *Bible* tells that a man named Noah (perhaps one of the first zoological environmentalists) had a big Ark in which he transported pairs of every kind of living creature safely over flood waters that covered the earth. He sent a raven out first, to scout for dry land (hurray for us!). He respected our intelligence, but the raven didn't return. Smart bird. Why should he leave paradise in favor of a noisy, undoubtedly odiferous, overcrowded Ark?! Doves were released next for the same purpose and they obediently returned.

In ancient Greece, both we and ravens were sacred birds of Apollo, god of the sun, healing, and prophecy. In Norse mythology, we were companions and minions of Odin, the father of all Gods. We would fly over land and sea acquiring news and then return to inform him of the world's activities. We had ignored the honorable Noah's request to return, but who would defy a god?

There is also an Australian aboriginal myth that, in the beginning of time, there were two powerful beings: an eagle and a crow. They were enemies and competitors. They both wielded spears, but the eagle made his spears with barbs pointing backward from the shaft. These weapons were less apt to be loosened from an impaled target. My kind was jealous. We plotted how to steal the eagle's secret. While the eagle was sound asleep, we snuck into his nest and absconded with his spear. Thus we learned how to copy the spear's "magic." To the Aborigines, we were, unfortunately, also associated with death. We wished to play with humans, but since they weren't inclined to respond during their lives (don't you think that's unfairly snooty?), we had to wait until after they had died. We were so misunderstood; we were only trying to have meaningful, cordial relationships!

The Tlingit people of Alaska told of their delight in our comedies. We had fun being humorously irreverent and ribald. We were believed to have created humans: one kingly Corvid tried twice to form humans out of rocks, but that took too long and was ridiculously difficult. Subsequently, he tried leaves, which were much easier. Then he proclaimed, "You are each like a leaf. You will grow to be beautiful, but you will soon fall off your branch and disintegrate on the ground. You will disappear." The great corvid had created life as well as death. Our contemporary murders enjoy this tale; our power was absolute!

American Indians imitated our dancing. We greeted travelers returning home or coming out of their homes. We were entertainers and companions; our personalities and intelligence bespoke similarities to these human friends. The Crow Nation of Montana was a plains tribe of rugged nomadic hunters. Their symbol was, and is, the eagle, but some early legends interpret the sacred large-beaked bird which hunted alongside them to be a crow. It was as clever and inured to the windy plains as they were, and sometimes led them to freshly killed buffalo and other edible animals.

The Irish goddess of war, Badb, could turn herself into a crow or raven and predict the outcome of a war. Following her instructions, we would gather at battlegrounds to wait for our subsequent banquet. Whichever side we congregated on determined the army that would lose. In the same vein, tales have been told that before the Battle of Agincourt in 1415 between the English, led by King Henry V, and the French, our corvid ancestors gathered on the French side, predicting that they would be defeated.

Pliny the Elder (an early Roman) recognized corvids in his work *Natural History.* He admired their cunning, their sophisticated abilities of communication, and their resourcefulness. He related a story of a raven that, during a drought, happened upon a bucket containing scarcely an inch of water, out of reach. He dropped stones into the bucket until the water had risen high enough to assuage his thirst. I believe that story. We are very intelligent, and our brain-to-body ratio is similar to a chimpanzee's and not too different from your own! We have large forebrains.

The soul of King Arthur of the Round Table is supposed to survive today as a crow or raven. It seems probable that his spirit inhabits *my* body! We know what royal leadership is all about!

We were appreciated in ancient Great Britain, notably during the 1400s and 1500s. King Henry VIII (1534) decreed that we were to be protected from hunters and Falconers. (Our eggs, however, were *not* protected; irrational idiocy!) In the 1500s our benefit to crops (more about that later), our janitorial services, warnings and superiority were duly recognized. The raven image was depicted on King Henry's royal shield and crest. However, when he had his second wife, Anne Boleyn (aka, "Midnight Crow") beheaded, English attitudes took an about-face. We now symbolized royal repression. Popular opinion took a nosedive throughout the next century. The English despised us because we fed on corpses from plagues and battlefields. (We didn't observe *them* cleaning up their messes!) Then, in the London fire of 1666, once again we scavenged so persistently that the remaining residents shrank from our presence, fearing that we were unclean and spread pestilence. They insisted that King Charles should slay us all, our offspring, eggs and every evidence of our existence! Think about that. It meant that their populace, from that time on, had to spend *their* time and effort doing what we had accomplished faster and with no fuss! We Corvidae *never* bother other beings out of spite, sport, or ignorance. I think that humans will forever adopt inane prejudices against one creature or another, or against one philosophy or another. (Alice becomes very disheartened concerning unfair thinking.) Though attitudes have now softened, we corvids have learned to be wary.

In Tibet, until the 1950s, "sky burials" were the usual send-offs for the population's deceased. The dead were carved into small pieces in reverential ceremonies, then laid out on altars for ravens, us, and other avian diners to partake of this offering. It was believed that we would carry the human souls and bodies into their next life. I don't know for sure, but I bet that was true; we're extremely skillful!

The poet, Lord Byron (1788-1824), though moody and dour, was a sensitively attentive animal lover. His companions consisted of dogs, cats, monkeys, peacocks, guinea hens, an eagle, a falcon, an Egyptian crane, and a crow of which he was particularly fond due to its intelligence and tomfoolery. Of course.

There are many poems written about us by famous men such as John Hay (who was secretary of state for presidents William McKinley and Teddy Roosevelt during the late 1800s and early 1900s). This one reminded Hay of his youthful years in Indiana:

The Crows at Washington (excerpt)

...*"The dim, deep air, the level ray*
Of dying sunlight on their plumes
Give them a beauty not their own;
Their hoarse notes fail and faint away;
A rustling murmur floating down
Blends sweetly with the thickening glooms;
They touch with grace the fading day,
Slow flying over Washington..."

Of course, though I don't like his death-image associations with us, I mustn't leave out my namesake Edgar Allan Poe's well-known poem *The*

Raven, inspired by his crow "familiar":

...Open here I flung the shutter, when, with many a flirt and flutter
In there stepped a stately Raven of the saintly days of yore
Not the least obeisance made he; not a minute stopped or stayed he
But with mien of lord or lady, perched above my chamber door
Perched upon a bust of Pallas just above my chamber door-perched and
sat and nothing more

Then this ebony bird beguiling my sad fancy into smiling,
By the grave and stern decorum of the countenance it wore,
"Though thy crest be shorn and shaven, thou," I said, "art sure no craven
Ghastly grim and ancient Raven wandering from the nightly shore
Tell me what thy lordly name is on the Night's Plutonian shore
"Quoth the raven "Nevermore."

There are six previous verses to this poem and eleven following, during which Poe expresses progressively wearier despair. I chose to quote the two verses that I found the most upbeat. (Poe was plagued by dependence on alcohol and fiercely mercurial, powerful mood swings.)

Douglas Anderson, a contemporary poet, wrote:

Crows
Hunch in the trees
to gossip
About God and his inexorable
experimenting,
about deer guts and fish so stupid
you could sell them air
and how out in the deserts
there's a dog called coyote
with their mind
but with no wings.
Crow with Iroquois hair.
Crow with a wisecrack
for everybody,
Crow with his beak
thrust through a bun,
the paper still clinging,
Crow in a midnight blue suit
standing in front of a judge:
Your Honor, I didn't

kill him,
just ate him
and I wasn't impressed.

I relish Mr. Anderson's acknowledgment of our humor!

Alice has a fondness for all books by Lewis Carroll (predictable); *Alice Through the Looking Glass* and *Alice's Adventures in Wonderland.* I quote:

Tweedledum and Tweedledee
Agreed to have a battle;
For Tweedledum said Tweedledee
Had spoiled his nice new rattle.
Just then flew down a monstrous crow,
As black as a tar-barrel;
Which frightened both the heroes so
They quite forgot their quarrel.

There were many more tales, beliefs and histories; too many to recount, but I will present one more that I find particularly interesting, and entertainingly factual.

As Esther Woolfson relates in her book, *Corvus: A life with Birds*, pgs. 111 and 112, Truman Capote, who wrote *Breakfast at Tiffany's* and *In Cold Blood*, had a pet raven named Lola:

...The account which appears in A Capote Reader was written twelve years after the winter when, living in Sicily in the early 1950s, Capote exchanged Christmas presents with the village girl, Graziella, who came to his house every day to cook and clean for him. He gave her a scarf, a sweater, and a necklace. She gave him a fledgling Raven that she had caught...Capote, who writes of his previous dislike and fear of birds, describes the Raven, as he first saw it, as both dreadful and pathetic, with severely clipped wings, black beak agape like the jaws of an idiot, its eyes flat and bleak...he shut it away in a spare room...Only in spring when one day the bird disappeared, did he realize, through his sense of loss, his affection for her, deciding in an instant that she was Lola, a name that " emerged like a new moon overhead."

She became a "princess," beloved by her master and indubitably the mistress of his two dogs. She rode around on the bulldog's back and ruled the household in general. To continue with Esther's rendition of Capote's story: ..."Lola was, like all Corvid, inclined to steal and cache. Among her prizes were the false teeth of an elderly guest, who was very upset, obliging Capote to find where it was that Lola cached her treasure: She leapt from floor to chair to bookshelf; then, as though it were a cleft in a mountain leading to Ali Baba's cavern, she squeezed between two books and disappeared behind them: evaporated like Alice through the looking glass. The Complete Jane Austin concealed her cache, which, when we found it, consisted, in addition to purloined dentures, of the long-lost keys to my car...a mass of paper money-thousands of lire torn into tiny scraps, as though intended for some future nest,-old letters, my best cuff links, rubber bands, yards of string, the first page of a short story I'd stopped writing because I couldn't find the first page, an American penny, a dry rose, a crystal button"...

I don't claim that any of these stories and fables are particularly important, nor does Alice deem them profound, but we both appreciate their evidence of my kind's eminence throughout the ages of man. We were, and still are, remarkable.

CURRENT OPINIONS AND ATTITUDES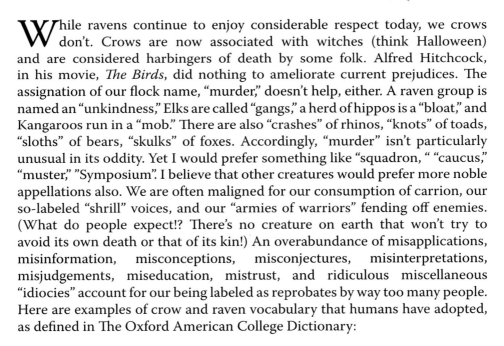

While ravens continue to enjoy considerable respect today, we crows don't. Crows are now associated with witches (think Halloween) and are considered harbingers of death by some folk. Alfred Hitchcock, in his movie, *The Birds*, did nothing to ameliorate current prejudices. The assignation of our flock name, "murder," doesn't help, either. A raven group is named an "unkindness," Elks are called "gangs," a herd of hippos is a "bloat," and Kangaroos run in a "mob." There are also "crashes" of rhinos, "knots" of toads, "sloths" of bears, "skulks" of foxes. Accordingly, "murder" isn't particularly unusual in its oddity. Yet I would prefer something like "squadron, " "caucus," "muster," "Symposium". I believe that other creatures would prefer more noble appellations also. We are often maligned for our consumption of carrion, our so-labeled "shrill" voices, and our "armies of warriors" fending off enemies. (What do people expect!? There's no creature on earth that won't try to avoid its own death or that of its kin!) An overabundance of misapplications, misinformation, misconceptions, misconjectures, misinterpretations, misjudgements, miseducation, mistrust, and ridiculous miscellaneous "idiocies" account for our being labeled as reprobates by way too many people. Here are examples of crow and raven vocabulary that humans have adopted, as defined in The Oxford American College Dictionary:

ravenous: to be exceedingly hungry (OK, I'll tolerate that one)

to rave: talk with irrational energy or to speak with enthusiasm or admiration

rave-up: a piece of pop music that is fun to dance to…Alice hasn't heard that one. (We crows do dance nearly as well as your aerobic and "zumba" enthusiasts.) I've never heard this particular phrase, either. It must belong to earlier human generations.

to crow: to express a feeling of happiness or triumph, as Peter Pan did).

crowbar: an iron bar with a flattened end used as a lever to open something (Yes, we do use tools and are clever problem-solvers. However, *humans* sometimes use crowbars as lethal weapons)

to eat crow: to be humiliated by having to admit one's defeat. (In my opinion, consuming us has nothing to do with humiliation. In past times and even to a small number of folk today, our flesh was/is delicious. Nevertheless, I urge you to sample *other* less deleterious foods.)

crow-bait: a horse that is near death (Yuck! how derogatory and such a skeletal creature would be too tough for my taste: though some of my compatriots might disagree.)

crows' feet: wrinkles, crinkles, and furrows. I have to admit that our feet aren't particularly fetching. However, compared to yours they are extremely functional.

Our raven cousins don't fare very well, either: How about rave, ravening, ravenous, unravel, ravish, ravage, etc.? Perhaps I have exaggerated just a bit the actual derivations of these words. However, though we are given recognition in your language, I resent the ones that I interpret as derogatory. Please accept my opinions with good-natured leniency rather than with the unreasonable *ravings* of an *old crow.*

OUR SANITARY NATURES

We preen often and thoroughly to stay clean, tidy, and glossy. (Have you noticed how iridescent our feathers are?) We preen each other, too. We have a particularly unique way to rid ourselves of parasites: we "ant." Eh-yah; we find anthills to lie on, crush the ants, and smear their juices onto our feathers, even under our wings. The ants possess formic acid and pungent anal fluids that are natural insecticides. (When you think about that, I guess it *is* a bit icky.) The live ants crawl onto our bodies to cart away lice and other parasites to feed their communities. Some avian experts think that the formic acid is also an intoxicant, except that it is not a drug like *your* intoxicants!

Compare our anting and sunning with an hour or two at a luxurious spa. Did I tell you about sunning? Well, on clear, warm days we lie flat on the ground with our wings spread and our beaks open to cool our sun drenched bodies. The sun turns our preening oils into a source of vitamin D. The heat also "revs up" parasites, which makes them easier to spot and pick off. We sometimes become so relaxed that we don't focus on the world around us. We "zone out". But unlike you, we don't have to worry about sticky sweat, chemically impregnated lotions, skin cancer or the effects of chemical bug sprays!

Rain doesn't bother us unless it is accompanied by stiff wind, thunder and lightning and/or cold temperatures. We love bathing in rain. (I'll say more about bathing later on.)

OUR "GOOD TASTE" BENEFITS THE WORLD

Isuppose you could consider us near-carnivores. Alice thinks we are omnivores. We eat multitudes of mosquitoes, gypsy moths, other biting insects, and arthropods. Don't go "Yuck!" Your Australians eat grubs and some people eat black ants, snakes (we eat only their livers), mice, scorpions and grind up rhinoceros horns thinking that the powder will be an aphrodisiac! The insects that we consume sometimes carry malaria and the dangerous West Nile virus. For people and cattle the West Nile parasites carry toxins that, when ingested, cause inflammation of the brain, weakness, lack of balance, and loss of cognition. Without medical intervention, death follows. Avian Flu virus can affect all mammals, including humans. Keep in mind that insects are the original culprits. I'd prefer that they take the blame.

We eat dead crabs that smell up your beaches, dead fish that wash ashore, and prickly sea urchins. Seagulls showed us how to drop the urchins and shellfish onto rocks to open them up. (There is a tiny island one hundred yards from Alice's house that we share with the gulls. She has named it "the smash and gorge rock".) Snake livers are a gourmet treat and believe it or not, river otter dung is also delicious! We eat grubs from your lawn, especially the Japanese Beetle ones. We've been accused of destroying large portions of your cornfields. Actually, we are primarily searching for and eating corn borers. We're doing farmers a favor in that respect, but I can understand why they are perturbed by our fondness for corn kernels. It's a dialectical problem! Alice says that researcher E.R. Kalmbach of the US Biological Survey (*In The Company of Crows and Ravens*, pg. 222) discovered that the stomachs of three corvids contained 85 May beetles, 72 wire worms, and 123 grasshoppers. He concluded that just one of us might feast upon up to 650 different food items a day!

> Consumption of corn borers by crows lowers this pest's over-winter survival yet does not damage growing corn, because the bugs are consumed during winter by migrant crows…a brood of four nestlings was fed 418 grasshoppers in a few hours…

Alice and her family don't grow corn, but her son, Chris, and his wife, MaryBeth, say that they have seen their murder eating their tomatoes, taking random bites and discarding the rest. I suspect that those crows are more interested in worms than tomato flesh. Well…I can't deny observation, but Alice and I can attest to the fact that we leave *her* tomatoes alone. She hasn't needed to shoo us away. We do eat her basil shoots, and accidentally uproot her young vegetables while we prod the earth for garden pests but she doesn't mind replanting.

We relish fast food: such as french fries and sandwich contents that litter your restaurant patios. We clean up under the tables where your children and some of you and your friends have picnics. We dine on restaurant backdoor discards, and leftovers in parking lots of delis, bakeries, and beaches. One more gourmet morsel that I'd like to tell you about to illustrate our "good taste": we like earthworms, but we're selective. We only consume the heads which contain their eggs, sperm (I don't lie!), brains, and gizzards. We discard the bodies, which are mostly intestines and waste. (Trivia: Did you know that regular garden earthworms have five "hearts"? Scientifically speaking, these are *aortic arches*.)

As I've mentioned before; because we eat carrion, we're unjustly spurned. Think twice: we're doing you a favor! (And many of *you* eat dead fish, beef, chickens, pigs, lambs, goose fat, calf brains, etc.) Your cars run over all sorts of rodents, foxes, raccoons, possums, deer, skunks, even your own pets! You shoot wild animals, take what you want of their bodies, and leave the rest. Wasteful! You try to teach your children not to litter, but I don't understand why many adults don't practice what they preach. We clean up many of your messes as well as our own. We're good recyclers!

We rub our bills on branches to keep them shiny and germ-free. Like raccoons, we often wash our food before eating it. We cache food that we can eat in the winter, but we don't leave perishable food hidden for long. Smart, huh? We crows have long black bills, curved on top and at the end. They are efficient tools for foraging, and eating, and I can carry more than one piece of food in an expandable pouch on the floor of my mouth (you have to use grocery bags).

How would you feel if you were taking a pleasant Sunday stroll and came upon a UFO (unidentifiable flattened object) or an IFO (identifiable) that had been on the hot sidewalk for a week or even just a day or two? Without our help it would become truly disgusting! Alice spotted a squirrel one day that lay lifeless in the hollow of a tree. It was still there the next day but not the third. No bones or mess visible. My cohorts had recycled it. We're efficient sanitary engineers and smart about it. You will rarely see a road-kill crow! If you do, it will undoubtedly be a young one that hasn't become street –wise. We have a "sixth sense" that warns us how much time we will have to dine between cars (even speeders)! We clean up carrion from even the very middle of your roads. Naturally, we avoid your highways and rush-hour congestions! One of Alice's unusual practices, which she should keep "under wraps", is to carefully relocate on-the-road corpses over to the sidelines or into brush, so that we don't have to endanger ourselves. Once in a while she takes the most intact ones back to her Moxie art studio and gallery to do sketches of.

If you have a quirky sense of humor, lay your child's dead goldfish, mouse, or hamster out on your lawn. It will be transported to its Nirvana expediently! You'll be providing a more fitting funeral ceremony than the much-used "flush"! Alice told me an amusing story about dead mice from when she was little: The tractor cutting down the wheat fields at her uncle's farm in Maine left a wake of deceased rodents. My kind was delighted, but Alice was grief-stricken. She gathered up a shoebox-full of the mice that weren't too mangled so she could give them a decent interment. However, she got diverted, probably by a game of "Spud" or "sardines," catching fireflies, or playing with the sheep which were apt to sneak into the house, not always by mistake. By the next morning, the mice smelled fetid. Thinking that they shouldn't go into the ground in such a putrid state, she poured her aunt's cherished bottle of Chanel#5 over their now sweetly fat little corpses (she was too young to know about bloat). After a solemn burial and an appreciative "bon voyage," they were forgotten. (Not forgotten by the dog, though, who dug them up!) As you've no doubt surmised, the missing bottle of perfume was *sorely* missed! The moral: Leave the dead mice to us!

PERSONALITY AND PROTECTION

Are we mean, dangerous, or marauding killers? Absolutely NOT! We *don't* kill sheep or cattle or their young, as some ranchers believe. They see a murder of us pecking at the carcass of a dead animal and draw the conclusion that we have killed it. We're simply "recycling" it as we're supposed to, and we will leave the ear-tag so they'll know which individual has died. Smart ranchers can then make an effort to figure out what actually caused the animal's death, such as an internal illness or coyote tooth scrapes on the bones. Though we are importantly beneficial, you may object to some of our proclivities: we eat other birds' eggs. However we actually take only about 6%. Consider *your* egg consumption, such as those of quail, ostrich, goose, sparrow (Alice informed me of this: she has a friend who fought in the Vietnam war. He was offered a sparrow, whole and feathered, surrounded by its eggs, as gourmet fare by a local resident.) People enjoy duck eggs and probably others that I don't know about. And, of course, chicken eggs.

We aren't mean but we naturally defend our nesting territories if we feel they are in jeopardy. Alice adhered a hawk's silhouette onto her picture window one time, to keep birds from hitting it. Since hawks are enemies, Tatters and I and one of our fledglings attacked it! (Sorry!). We protect our ill and/or wounded comrades who are in vulnerable locations. We feed our sick and injured, and gather around a dying comrade, offering safety and warmth. We stay until it reaches its end. We hover near it for a while, and then take our leave. Alice says that's what most humans do, too.

We remember family members who have migrated to other murders, and we won't fight our "homies", even when we compete for the same territory (though we usually do respect domain boundaries, we often do squabble about them). During cold winters, several murders will come together for hunting, and communal warmth at night. We attack marauders such as eagles, owls, and the large hawks that could kill us, eat our young and eggs, and compete for our food. Often our neighbors will join us. We will defend ourselves against (or hide from) possums, weasels, raccoons, and nearly all humans. Our strategy is to dive-bomb an enemy and/or gang up on it, flapping at its body and, when necessary, pecking at its wings, tail feathers, and especially its head. We only attack humans when they are too near to or damaging our nesting places. We might attack if they have been hazardous to us first (our intention is to *chase away* danger, not to kill.) Every organism in the world protects itself and its young in one way or another.

I feel that I should point out that humans are capable of *extreme* savagery, murder, and mayhem. There are big-game heads mounted on some of your walls. You trap for fur, fox-hunt with dogs and seem to enjoy other barbaric activities that I don't approve of. We never kill for pleasure, and we never kill each other. We have no true bird friends except within our own murders, but we're tolerant. You humans are inconsistent. On one hand, you've established that we are to be protected by law under the Migratory Bird Treaty Act. Commendable! We and our raven cousins are protected in Scotland by the Wildlife and Countryside Act. (Smart folks, those Scots!) On the other hand, in this country, we are regularly "controlled" by federal agents and hunted simply for sport during the seasons when you can't find other targets. *Why?* You don't even gather up our dead bodies We receive neither eulogy nor honor! Occasionally, we're killed for *food* by humans, but that's often due to extreme hunger.

We do each have an angel and a devil within us. We crows call the latter *humor*. If you leave your diamond ring out on the garden post, we might take it, just as Lola did. We might adorn our nests with bracelets, shiny watches (we love "bling")… ribbon, Christmas tree tinsel, coins, grocery lists, children's small stuffed animals. We steal balls from your golf courses. They look like eggs. We'll test the flavor of garden seeds if you leave them out in the open. We love basil and parsley shoots. (Deer, raccoons, rabbits, et al., do significantly more damage to your plants than we do.) Alice holds tight to her research notes when she is outside, suspecting that, though we don't eat that stuff, we might decorate our nests with it or stash it away.

Alice had an acquaintance who saved a baby crow and named it, unimaginatively, "Crow." It survived happily to adulthood within his family and home territory, sometimes riding on his shoulder, coming when it was called, and following him around. Crow had a sense of humor that wasn't always appreciated. He liked to pull clothespins off of the laundry line *after* the clean clothes and sheets were hung. He often rang the gong on the back porch, ate the chickens' eggs when he could get at them, and fed at the bird feeder (I do too, and why not? Get used to it-we're birds!) Crow's greetings were enthusiastic even with strangers, some of whom cowered in fear, misunderstanding that he was only trying to bid them welcome. Eventually and tragically, an unkind, intolerant neighbor shot him. I rest my case concerning savagery.

OUR SOCIAL LIVES

We cluck, trill, and sing to each other, especially in early spring when many of us feel romantic or desire companionship. We caw gently to keep track of each other. One murder may have caws that others don't share. We *do* share the same vocabulary when we want to gather together. Those of us who are mated may even articulate tones and mannerisms that aren't used by other crows. When we are wooing each other, we grab each other's bills (kinda' like your kissing). The ornithologists call that "allobilling." We "allopreen" each other's faces and heads. We bring each other gifts, food, and treasures. Last April (our mating time), Alice watched me puff up my breast feathers. She thought I looked like a muscle man or magistrate announcing "look at me! See how elegant and stalwart I am!" (I agreed with her-I am the Monarch, after all!) Tatters and I followed each other around or stood together wing-to-wing. I wouldn't let her out of my sight, and chastised other males who came too close to her. I'd "coo" and "cuckoo" and "rattle" with her (our style of "sweet nothings"). We'd crouch with our wings out horizontally, drooping while vibrating our tails. We might scream when we consummate our partnership. (Alice, being frank, commented to a friend that our processes were quite anthropomorphic. Do you think so too?)

My murder and I often follow the same daily routines. These, much of the time, involve preening, then breakfast, then scouting and hunting, then feeding again-taking into account low tide times, which offer excellent feasts-and, of course, sleeping (we tuck our heads under the feathers on our backs or bow our heads). From the middle of March through June, those of us who are mated spend a great deal of time and effort feeding our young! We become *really* fed up (no pun intended) with our lazy offspring who just sit on tree branches pleading for free food every minute, even when they are nearly adults and can fly. (Alice tires of their constant demands also, and she imagines that the whole neighborhood feels the same!) Getting back to facts: Our one-and two-year-olds find their own food and often one of them stays to baby-sit and help feed their parents' next brood.

Fortunately, somewhere amidst our routines, we all play. Our cavorting includes hops, one-foot-forward skips (two-legged cantering), and leaps. One of our games is to grab an object (piece of paper, ball, small stuffed animal, etc.), rise into the air with it, then drop it for another crow (or ourselves) to swoop down and snatch. Sometimes we try to catch it in midair. While Alice gazed out of her window one afternoon, she noticed one of our offspring sitting on the porch rail "churring." A sibling swooped down and placed a leaf at the other's feet. That crow then picked it up and flew away...gift or a game? We play keep-away once in a while, in earnest. Our offspring do sometimes get "testy" with each other, as human youngsters do. Alice has seen us poke at each other, signaling "move over!" or "my turn!" or "I get first choice!" We also poke just for the game of it. We love ground-tag, and you've seen us play air-tag, I'm sure. When our young are learning to fly, we demonstrate rapid descents, steep climbs, banks, graceful swoops, well-calculated landings, and from-standing takeoffs. These lessons are fun for all of us. We enjoy watching our offspring practice, and are attentive to their need for more coaching.

While perched in the trees, sharing branches, we side-step toward and away from each other. We play follow-the-leader and tug-of-war. We splash in puddles, bird baths and, indeed, any pool of water, preferably in the morning after preening. Heated birdbaths are a treat in winter, for amusement, washing, and drinking. Though you don't drink the water in your baths, you enjoy your hot-tubs in the same way. Also in winter, we flutter in the snow. You can see where we've played. We make our own type of snow-angels. We even slide down snowbanks and hillsides, repeating the game over and over again. As you know, we don't swim, however, after watching the antics of Alice's grandchildren at the beach, and being the gamester that I am, I wish I could! Once in a while, we tease other animals, especially your tame ones. My murder and I like to swoop down at Alice's English setter, Millie, who ignores us. She has kindly tolerated us and accompanied Alice as she follows and watches us.

COURTING AND PARENTING

As pairs, we have strong bonds. As parents, we are synchronized, protective and attentive.

We start courting in the early spring with a great deal of flirting. Our females "display" more than males. I'm sure you can identify with that. We allopreen, rub our beaks together, coo, "dance" for each other, fluff our feathers, and bob, etc. I think I have mentioned those tender affections before. We males love to demonstrate our aerial skills. (We can be as macho as many of your own males!) We often start mating in March and immediately begin building our nests. Here in Maine and in other cold-winter climates some of us wait until April. Our females choose our nest sites, preferring cedar and dense evergreen trees. Cedar bark has a natural insecticide, as you know: you have cedar closets and trunks to deter moths and other cloth and fur-chewing pests. Our mates often peel the bark off of these trees to line our nests so that our offspring will benefit. Most evergreen trees offer protection, canopy, and camouflage among their dark branches (deciduous trees don't comply with any of our specifications). Once again, our females are the most competent architects, using moss, fur from dead animals, feathers, twigs, bits of yarn, string, tinsel, and torn paper. (Alice left some of these things out in her field last spring. Even though it's soft and fluffy, she knew not to leave laundry lint for us, as it has chemicals in it that make us and our babies ill.) We males help by gathering twigs and other building supplies, but we do very little of the construction. If one of our yearlings has stayed with us, it pitches in to help. We are careful not to be seen during this process. Our nests are, on average, two to three feet wide and about six inches deep. If we detect that we are being watched, we'll fly to a different tree, not returning to our own until danger is past.

After we have consummated our mating, the females usually lay four to eight pale cerulean, rusty-brown speckled eggs. The incubation period lasts a month, give or take a week. Our nestlings are born, with their eyes closed, heavy-headed, with potbellied stomachs, naked, thin-skinned, helpless, and *hungry*: there are no beauty contest winners among them. They weigh less than an ounce: imagine fourteen potato chips. We bring food to our females while they sit on the nests and nurture our nestlings. (*Nestling*: any young bird that can't fly or leave the nest.) Here's a fact that your own species will find grossly fascinating: our babies "relieve themselves" into sacs that their bodies manufacture, and plop them into the nest. The parents pick up the "packages" and fly them quite a distance away to places where they can be relinquished in secret. When the fledglings grow, they toss their own sacs over the nest edge. Your children use a toilet, a very sanitary and effortless process! Though baby crows deposit "dropables," *that* procedure is just as fastidious, "green" (easily biodegradable, and, in fact, "off the grid") as your system.

By the fifth day after hatching, nestlings' eyes are open. (Though it is difficult for humans to examine the color of a crow's eye, we have black pupils and dusty purple irises: beautiful!) In just ten or eleven days, feathers start becoming visible. The little ones have become *fledglings*. In three to four weeks, they leave the nest but stick around near their parents for care and "home schooling." They seem (to your eyes) just like us, but if you look carefully, you'll see that they are less shiny and have a brownish hue to their "black" feathers, especially on their backs. Their tails and wings are a tad shorter than ours, even though their bodies are full-size.

Your species sometimes gives birth to albinos. We do also, but it is extremely rare, and they are often killed during their first year because they have no camouflage and black feathers are stronger than less pigmented ones. An albino's feathers are dangerously weak. Once in a while, we grow white feathers just here or there. They are the results of bad wounds or other skin damage. Life can sometimes be tough for us!

More than half of our broods (offspring that are born and raised in one season) die in their first year, and a third of them leave their home turf to wander or join other murders. One in five stays with his parents (yes, usually a male!). He helps by protecting his parents, foraging for food, gathering nesting materials, and baby-sitting. I guess your sons are often like that, too. Certainly, Alice's son is close by to help. Though her daughter lives farther away, she would come if Alice was in trouble, and their mates would, too! Alice is lucky! By their second year our sons leave to find mates. A few breed in their second year, but most breed when they are three. A young crow's brain is as well developed as ours are; they are just as intelligent, but they are *not* streetwise. Literally! They sit on roads to eat or sun, not realizing how dangerous speeding vehicles are. They aren't wary enough of cats and other enemies. You'll find more dead young crows in late summer and early fall but fewer in late fall and winter. To gain experience and wisdom for a better chance of survival, they must heed our warnings and follow our example. Luckily, they learn fast. We hope they graduate with honors.

We live, if "durable," five to seven years. *So very brief our reign,* says Alice, sadly. Our deaths are usually caused by predators, starvation, cold, injury, defects, and diseases, and, of course, senescence. We are as vulnerable to fateful vicissitudes as all other creatures! Speaking of starvation…it is now dead low tide and I must leave you shortly to go seek the crustaceans (crabs, out-of-their-shells hermit crabs, horse-shoe crabs, small shrimp, etc.), mussels, sea worms, minnows and lobster detritus, all of which I find nourishing and absolutely delicious.

IN CONCLUSION

I hope you have been pleasantly fascinated and respectfully inspired by this book and will pay more attention to us now. My opinions have been mine alone, and you've undoubtedly realized that I'm utterly, subjectively, biased- though Alice's contributions to this little tome are based on factual research and on her observations of, and friendship with, me. She has asked me to request your generous latitude if you believe that any of our testimony is in error. Alice has made a concerted effort to bring to you an honest account of our Being. I shall let her speak for herself:

To all of you who are reading this-family, friends, interested strangers...

I thank you sincerely for your indulgence, and truly hope that the reading of this book has amused and informed you! Isn't Edgar a true egotist, though? I'm fond of him, however, and will continue to be taught by him and his murder.

As for my research...I've gone about it the "I once was a teenager" way, spending quiet, soothing, book-scented hours in the Yarmouth library, carting borrowed books back and forth, and writing assorted "gleanings" down on file cards, then dividing them by "chapters" and arranging them in my mother's old use-polished, pine file box. Bowing to current technology, my computer, named "Jabberwock" (as in "beware the Jabberwock" from Lewis Carroll's *Through the Looking-Glass*), has done the duty of composing a distinct improvement over the write-and-erase-on-yellow-lined-paper– then–attempt-a-final-type-up system of the past. However, I'm not fond of my computer. In general, I dislike the whole do-it-fast nature of new technology and new-generation efficiencies. (I have to admit that I do admire how proficient and enthusiastic our "heirs" are at it!) Yet I've happily accomplished in eight months what would originally have taken me a year and a half and resulted in illegible script, soda-stained papers, and an addiction to No-Doz.

I offer, on a personal note, many thanks for the support and interest of my family (they find me oddly amusing):

Thank you Christopher and MaryBeth Lorenz, little William, and Lucia for your patience with me…Chris, you once asked, "Mom, what's your target market?" and I answered "Santa Claus and my neighbors who also know Edgar." Your simple question helped me realize that I really *was* writing with a purpose! I also thank my daughter, Ana Dierkhising, and her family-Adam, Ben, and Elsa; my brother, Tim Ingraham, his all-heart wife, Joannie (their interest in birds I have long admired and found inspirational), and sons Alex and Sam (who speaks fluent Latin).

I've received considerable encouragement, spelling advice and wording from Craig Hurd and his son, Connor. Dori Salzman has kept me sane (I hope to be like her when I grow up). To Jim Thatcher: You've gone out of your way to offer inspiration, wisdom, and editing advice, as have Meryl Mills and Bruce Lancester. I'm heartfully grateful. My next-door neighbors, the Daniels and Elliotts, have been patient and tolerant of Edgar's murder and my "shenanigans" with them. Thank you, David, for your photographic expertise, and Edgar has asked me to apologize for scaring your family with his attacks on the alien crows that he sees in your windows.

Most important of all, thank you, **Edgar, Tatters, Shy, Greedy, Scrappy, Sometimes,** and the new young members, **Hi,** and **Hi.** (I can't tell those two apart…yet.)

Felix qui potuit rerum cognoscere causus (Virgil)*
Noscam dedat veritam, veritas nunquam perit et Corvidae nunquam perit! (Sam Ingraham)**

*Happy is he who has been able to know the reason for things (Virgil)
**Knowledge gives truth, truth never dies, and Corvidae never die!

REFERENCES

I give "Mt. Everest" credit to the authors of the volumes that I've read, and apologize for not doing *ibids* for each piece of information: many of you have duplicated each other's data.

Bradley, James V: *Crows and Ravens:* New York: InfoBase Publishing, 2006.

Bradley, James V. *Nature Walk: Crows and Ravens*: New York: Chelsea Clubhouse/Infobase Publishing,2002.

Chatterjee, Sancar: *The Rise of Birds: 225 MillionYears of Evolution*: Baltimore: Johns Hopkins University Press,

Feduccia, Jay Alan *The Origin and Evolution of Birds*: New Haven: Yale University Press, 2000.

Haupt, Lyanda Lynn *Crow Planet-Essential Wisdom from the Urban Wilderness* :.New York: Little, Brown & Co., 2009.

Heinrich, Bernard, *Ravens in Winter*: New York, Summit Books, 1999

Johnson, Sylvia *Crows:* Minneapolis: Lerner Publishing Group, 2005.

Kilham, Lawrence *The American Crow and Common Raven*: College Station, Texas, Texas A&M University Press, c. 1989

Marzluff, John M. and Tony Angell: *In The Company of Crows and Ravens*: 2005: New Haven, Yale University Press..

Oxford American College Dictionary :New York: 2002 : G.P. Putnam's Sons, and Oxford University Press, Berkeley, CA..

Pringle, Lawrence, *Listening to the Crows:* 1976.: New York : Cromwell Co.,

Savage, Candace, *Crows: Encounters with the Wise Guys of the Avian World*: 2005: Vancouver/Toronto/Berkeley: Douglas & McIntyre Publishing Group.

Woolfson Esther, *Corvus; A Life with Birds*: 2009: Berkeley: Counterpoint Press,.

"*Crow Poem*" by Douglas Anderson from *Blues For Unemployed Secret Police: Poems,*_Curbstone Press, Willimantic, Conn.

"*Dust of Snow*" by Robert Frost, (1923), from *The Poetry of Robert Frost*, edited by Edward C. Latham, New York: Henry Holt and Company., 2005.

"*The Raven*" from *Poe: Poetry and Tales*,New York: Literary Classics of the United States, Inc., New York, N.Y., 1984